POWERFUL PREDATORS

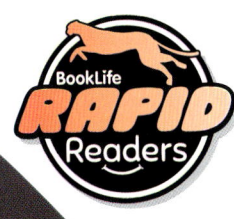

BRUTAL BIRDS

All rights reserved.
Printed in China.

A catalogue record for this book is available from the British Library.

ISBN: 978-1-80505-011-7

Written by:
Mignonne Gunasekara
Adapted by:
Charis Mather
Edited by:
Rebecca Phillips-Bartlett
Designed by:
Drue Rintoul

©2023
BookLife Publishing Ltd.
King's Lynn, Norfolk
PE30 4LS, UK

All facts, statistics, web addresses and URLs in this book were verified as valid and accurate at time of writing. No responsibility for any changes to external websites or references can be accepted by either the author or publisher.

AN INTRODUCTION TO BOOKLIFE RAPID READERS...

Packed full of gripping topics and twisted tales, BookLife Rapid Readers are perfect for older children looking to propel their reading up to top speed. With three levels based on our planet's fastest animals, children will be able to find the perfect point from which to accelerate their reading journey. From the spooky to the silly, these roaring reads will turn every child at every reading level into a prolific page-turner!

CHEETAH

The fastest animals on land, cheetahs will be taking their first strides as they race to top speed.

MARLIN

The fastest animals under water, marlins will be blasting through their journey.

FALCON

The fastest animals in the air, falcons will be flying at top speed as they tear through the skies.

PHOTO CREDITS

IMAGES ARE COURTESY OF SHUTTERSTOCK.COM. WITH THANKS TO GETTY IMAGES, THINKSTOCK PHOTO AND ISTOCKPHOTO. RECURRING – AMOVITANIA. COVER – NOTIONPIC. 4–5 – NOAH SYDNOR, ELENA BLANES 6–7 – VADIM PETRAKOV, RICHARD CONSTANTINOFF. 8–9 – ANDY WASLEY, MARTIN HIBBERD. 10–11 – FERNANDO SANCHEZ, ROBERT ADAMEC. 12–13 – BARBARA ASH, CHARIDY BUNSA. 14–15 – ERNI, DILOMSKI. 16–17 – CDK PHOTOS, MARTINE LIU 58. 18–19 – PETER WEY, BCBIMAGES. 20–21 – CHRIS HILL, HARRY COLLINS PHOTOGRAPHY. 22–23 – SCOTT MIRROR, BIRDIEGAL, MIKE VAN KAL.

CONTENTS

PAGE 4	Welcome to the World of Predators
PAGE 6	Guzzling Great White Pelicans
PAGE 8	Killer Common Kestrels
PAGE 10	Beastly Barn Owls
PAGE 12	Savage Secretary Birds
PAGE 14	Scary Great Skuas
PAGE 16	Cunning Common Kingfishers
PAGE 18	Eager Bald Eagles
PAGE 20	Frightful Peregrine Falcons
PAGE 22	Brutal and Beastly
PAGE 24	Glossary and Index

Words that look like <u>this</u> are explained in the glossary on page 24.

WELCOME to the World of PREDATORS

In the animal world, predators are everywhere.

Predators hunt other animals for food and are terrifying to their <u>prey</u>!

Birds might be beautiful, but some of them can also be beastly.

Get ready to meet some brutal birds.

Guzzling Great White PELICANS

Great white pelicans are large birds that live in watery areas.

They are known for the stretchy pouches under their bills.

Great white pelicans hunt by swimming together.

They circle fish so that they cannot escape. Then, they scoop them up.

KILLER Common
KESTRELS

Kestrels are not the biggest birds, but they are still dangerous hunters.

They eat other small animals, including some birds.

Common kestrels can <u>hover</u> in one spot in the air. This helps them see prey from above.

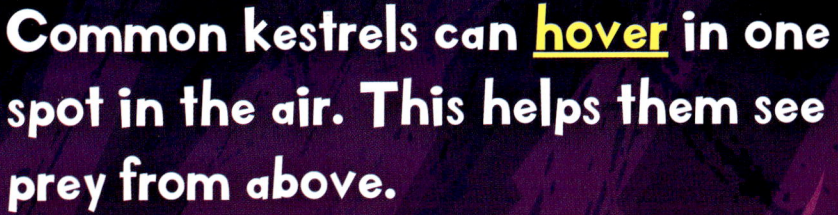

BEASTLY Barn OWLS

Barn owls are most active at night. Their excellent hearing helps them find prey, even in the dark.

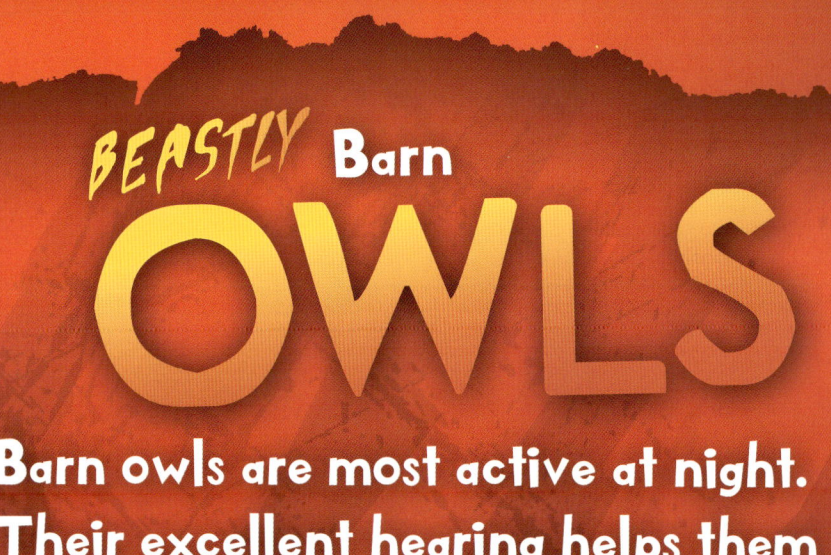

Barn owls can fly very quietly to sneak up on prey.

They attack with their hooked beaks and sharp <u>talons</u>.

SAVAGE Secretary BIRDS

Unlike most birds, secretary birds do not hunt from the air.

They stomp on the grass to find and chase prey.

Secretary birds attack with their short beaks and powerful feet. They might even stomp on their prey to kill them.

SCARY Great SKUAS

The <u>coast</u> is home to lots of birds, including the great skua.

This large seabird has a sharp beak and talons.

Great skuas are known for stealing food from other birds.

They will fly angrily at people to protect their nests.

CUNNING Common KINGFISHERS

A good place to find common kingfishers is near slow-moving water.

They mostly hunt for small fish and sometimes eat insects.

Common kingfishers spot fish by sitting on <u>perches</u> near the water. Then, they dive in to catch their prey.

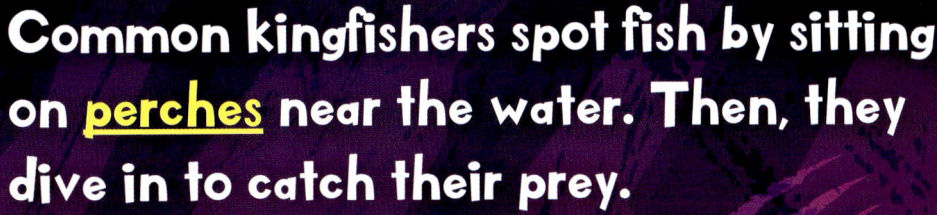

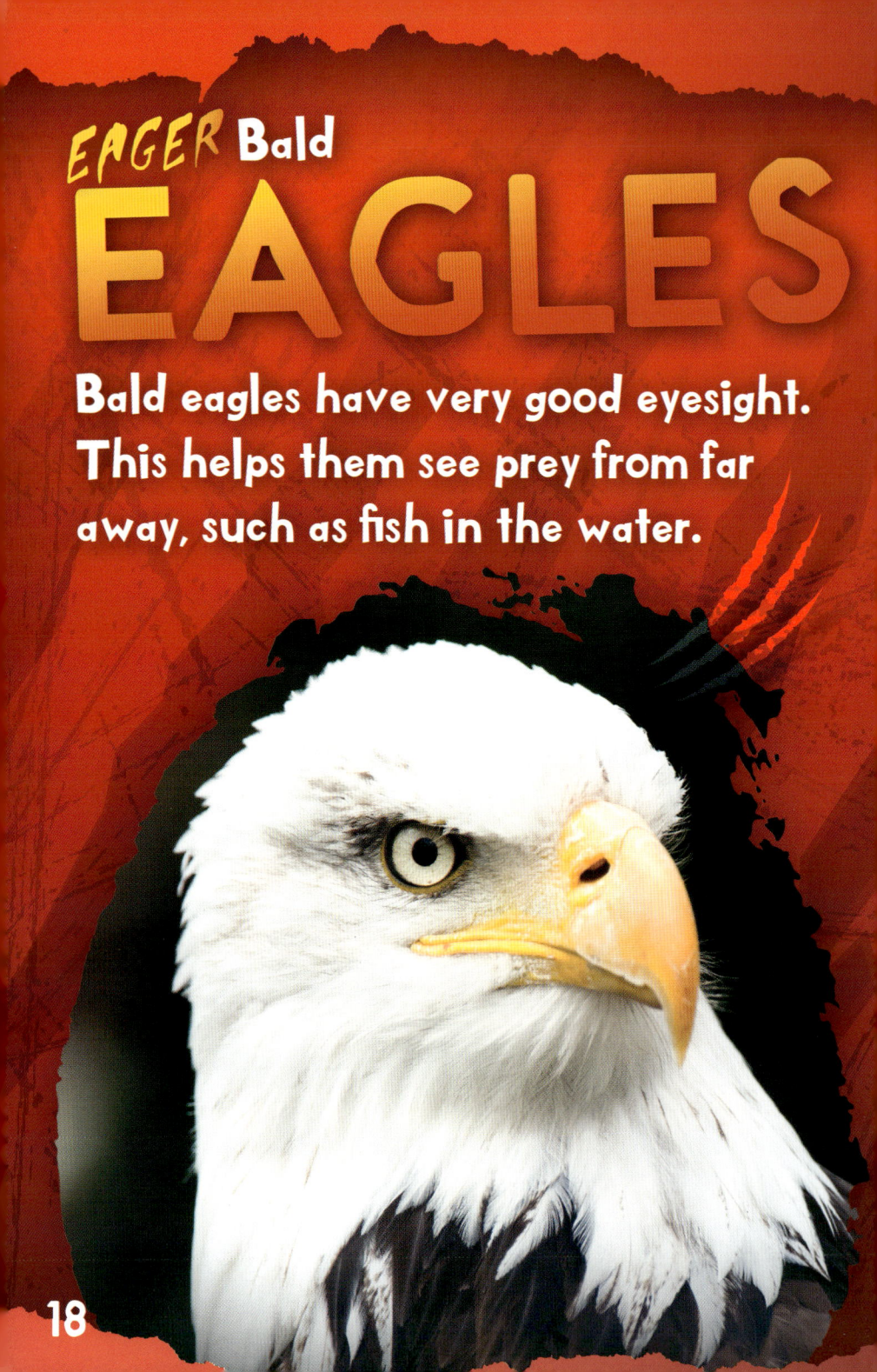

Eager Bald EAGLES

Bald eagles have very good eyesight. This helps them see prey from far away, such as fish in the water.

They use their long, sharp talons to grab fish.

Then, they rip into them with their hooked beaks.

FRIGHTFUL Peregrine FALCONS

Peregrine falcons mainly hunt other birds, such as pigeons.

These falcons grab their prey out of the air with their talons.

A hunting peregrine falcon can dive towards its prey at speeds of over 300 kilometres per hour.

BRUTAL and BEASTLY

These powerful predators are all birds, but they all hunt in very different ways.

Some snatch prey from the skies.

22

Some scoop prey from the sea.

Some grab prey on the ground.

They are all brutal in their own way!

GLOSSARY

COAST — the area where land and sea meet

HOVER — to float in the air

PERCHES — places where birds can rest

PREY — animals that are hunted by other animals for food

TALONS — claws

INDEX

AIR 9, 12, 20

BEAKS 11, 13–14, 19

FISH 7, 16–19

PREY 4, 9–13, 17–18, 20–23

TALONS 11, 14, 19–20

WATER 6, 16–18